"Amy J. L. Baker and Katherine C. Andre have written this practical and child-friendly book to help children learn resilience for coping with divorce and other difficult interpersonal situations. They focus on the real experiences of divorce from the standpoint of the child. Through brief, structured written activities and a tone of kindness and support, they offer your child a chance to work through their experiences with self-awareness and a sense of competence."

—**Jeffrey Zimmerman, PhD, ABPP**, psychologist who specializes in working with families of divorce, mediator and collaborative divorce professional, and coauthor of *The Co-parenting Survival Guide* and *Adult Children of Divorce*

"Getting Through My Parents' Divorce is a very important and timely book. Written by two experts in the field, this book provides detailed, hands-on guidance for children struggling to make sense of the often chaotic and overwhelming feelings that can result from divorce. I highly recommend it."

—**Joshua Coleman, PhD**, psychologist and author of *When Parents Hurt: Compassionate Strategies When You and Your Grown Child Don't Get Along*

"This is an excellent workbook for children whose parents are separated or divorced. As I read *Getting Through My Parents' Divorce*, I wondered how this book will come into the hands of youngsters who will benefit from it. Perhaps therapists or school counselors will give this book to children from divorced families. The authors, Amy J. L. Baker and Katherine C. Andre, suggest that a parent could give this workbook to his or her child and perhaps help the child with some of the activities. Even better, let's hope that in some families, the divorcing parents will join together in providing this book to their child—and all of them will find valuable lessons in its pages."

—**William Bernet, MD**, Professor Emeritus in the department of psychiatry at Vanderbilt University School of Medicine, Nashville, TN

"Divorce is a family crisis. *Getting Through My Parents' Divorce* is a series of lessons for children to strengthen their resolve, learn effective coping skills, and avoid the pitfalls of self-blame and divided loyalties."

—**Douglas Darnell, PhD**, CEO of PsyCare, Inc., and author of *Divorce Casualties*

"Baker and Andre have created a workbook that speaks to children who are experiencing the sadness, anger, and confusion of divorce. Oftentimes a child's voice is silenced through the divorce process. *Getting Through My Parents' Divorce* allows their voices to be heard loud and clear. This workbook should be in the hands of every child of divorce in hopes that it will contribute to healing, which will produce mature, responsible adults. This workbook will fill children with confidence, trust, and self-esteem. This would be a priceless gift for any child who could benefit from the character-building skills offered by the authors. [This book] will change a life today so that we all have a better tomorrow!"

—**Mayor Jill Egizii**, president of the Parental Alienation Awareness Organization

Getting Through My Parents' Divorce

A Workbook for Children Coping
with Divorce, Parental Alienation,
and Loyalty Conflicts

AMY J. L. BAKER, PhD
KATHERINE C. ANDRE, PhD

Instant Help Books
An Imprint of New Harbinger Publications, Inc.

Publisher's Note

This publication is designed to provide accurate and authoritative information in regard to the subject matter covered. It is sold with the understanding that the publisher is not engaged in rendering psychological, financial, legal, or other professional services. If expert assistance or counseling is needed, the services of a competent professional should be sought.

Distributed in Canada by Raincoast Books

Copyright © 2015 by Amy J. L. Baker and Katherine Andre
Instant Help Books
An Imprint of New Harbinger Publications, Inc.
5674 Shattuck Avenue
Oakland, CA 94609
www.newharbinger.com

Cover design by Amy Shoup
Acquired by Melissa Kirk
Edited by James Lainsbury

Library of Congress Cataloging-in-Publication Data

Baker, Amy J. L.
  Getting through my parents' divorce : a workbook for children coping with divorce, parental alienation, and loyalty conflicts / Amy J.L. Baker and Katherine Andre.
    pages cm
  ISBN 978-1-62625-136-6 (paperback) -- ISBN 978-1-62625-137-3 (pdf e-book) -- ISBN 978-1-62625-138-0 (epub)
1. Children of divorced parents--Juvenile literature. 2. Divorce--Psychological aspects--Juvenile literature. I. Andre, Katherine. II. Title.
  HQ777.5.B344 2015
  306.89--dc23

                          2015005423

Printed in the United States of America

17   16   15

10   9   8   7   6   5   4   3   2   1   First printing

Contents

Note to Caring Adults

If you are reading this book, it is probably because you care about a child whose family is splitting up or is in conflict. Divorce and conflict are stressful experiences for everyone involved. Children experience strong feelings that can overwhelm them and interfere with their social and emotional well-being.

In most circumstances, parents are able to help their children cope with day-to-day challenges. When parents split up, however, their own struggles can interfere with their ability to help their children.

Some children of divorce feel angry, hurt, worried, confused, guilty, sad, or afraid. Often these children feel responsible for their parents' breakup. They may keep their feelings inside, and they may think they are bad kids. We created this workbook to teach children how to manage and cope with the strong feelings that arise when parents divorce. The rules and tools they learn in this workbook will help them love and feel loved by both parents. They will become more resilient and will develop skills for facing challenges throughout their lives.

As a caring adult, you can help not only by giving a child this workbook but by lending an ear. A caring conversation might start with asking about the activities in the workbook, or asking to help with some of them. The most important thing is to show that you care and are available to listen and talk about thoughts and feelings.

By offering to listen and guide, you can make a difference in a child's life. You can help the child love and feel loved by both parents. Thank you for wanting to help.

Note to Parents

Divorce is not an easy process for a parent. You are going through a lot of changes, and your stress level may be higher than ever. Conversations with the other parent can escalate into shouting and fighting, responsibilities increase, time seems in shorter supply, emotional resources become limited, and conflict abounds. Parents can be overwhelmed, and kids sometimes receive the fallout of all of the tension and conflict. Children often blame themselves and think they are somehow responsible. Children of divorce can experience a range of strong emotions, including anger, confusion, fear, sadness, guilt, hurt, and worry.

It's best if parents can be role models to resolve conflict without fighting, but sometimes that's not possible. Unfortunately, kids start to wonder, *If my parents can't solve their problems, how can I solve mine? If my parents are fighting, maybe I am to blame.* When kids don't receive help during a divorce, they may carry these feelings and thoughts with them for years.

We created this workbook to help kids manage all the strong feelings that get stirred up when parents don't get along. This book can help you help your child when you may not be at your parenting best. Little mistakes can loom large for parents going through divorce. (For parenting advice see *Co-parenting with a Toxic Ex* by Baker and Fine, 2014.) Kids can work through the activities alone or with a caring adult, such as a counselor or you. If you do the workbook with your child, make sure you allow the child to set the pace without any pressure, expectation, or judgment. There is no rule or goal for how many activities the child should do in any one sitting. We want the workbook to be fun and engaging, not a chore to get through. Please be sure to allow your child to answer the questions and do the exercises; your child will gain the most from the workbook that way. Your suggestions or ideas can influence the way your child processes feelings.

Divorce and family conflict are hard on everyone, but the rules and tools children learn in this workbook will help them become resilient and will provide skills they can use to handle difficult situations later in life. Remember, the most important thing is that your child knows you are there for him or her. This workbook is one way to show that you care.

Welcome to Your Workbook!

This workbook is about what can happen inside you when your parents are getting divorced. It can be hard when parents fight, and you may have lots of feelings about that. These feelings may be stressing you out in a big way.

The upset you feel inside when your parents fight has different names. This workbook will help you name and cope with these feelings. When you notice and name a feeling, you start to feel better. It is easier to be okay with a feeling when you know what it is and trust that you can deal with it.

This workbook will also help you know yourself and think for yourself. You cannot control what your parents do. But you can control how you react. You can learn to be strong and think for yourself. Then, with new tools, you can choose to cope in a new and better way. When you think for yourself, you can stay out of parent problems and avoid doing things that aren't right for you. Not only will this workbook help you deal with your parents' divorce, it will help you with other problems you may face now and later in life.

It is not easy to have parents fighting and getting divorced, but you can get through this. You will learn rules and tools in this workbook that help, and you can find caring adults to talk to about your feelings. You have a right to be happy. You have a right to love and feel loved by both parents.

In this workbook you will learn:

1. How to identify and understand your feelings

2. Rules for loving and feeling loved by both parents

3. Coping tools to help you follow the rules

You Are Not Alone

Jenny is a ten-year-old girl. She has a younger brother and an older sister. Her parents used to fight a lot, and then last year they divorced. Her father moved out and she only sees him on weekends and Wednesday nights. Every time her dad picks her up her parents have an argument about money or the schedule. Jenny thought the yelling would stop after her dad moved out, but it hasn't.

Mike is ten. His mom lives in an apartment with her mother. His dad lives in an apartment with his new girlfriend. Mike has two older brothers. The three boys spend about half their time with each parent. Mike's parents act like they hate each other and argue all of the time about schedules, especially now that Mike takes karate three times a week and joined the swim team.

Maria and Miguel are eleven-year-old twins who live with their dad. Any time their mom shows up at school or basketball practice, the two parents have a big fight. When both parents are at school games, Maria and Miguel feel like they can't go over to their mom because their dad gets mad. The last time that happened, their dad told them it was time for them to choose. He wanted them to tell the judge that they don't like and don't feel safe with their mom anymore.

These kids are all dealing with parents who divorced and don't get along. It can be hard for kids when their parents fight. It can be hard staying out of parent problems. We know from experience that kids whose parents fight sometimes have a hard time loving and feeling loved by both parents. We want to help you with that by sharing some rules.

- Remember the truth about both parents

- Make good choices

- Make yourself proud

- Be brave

- Keep trying

- Get the help you need

- Take care of your mind and body

Having divorcing and fighting parents can be tough! It can be hard to follow the rules. That's why we are going to give you the tools that will help you love and feel loved by both parents.

Remember the Truth About Both Parents

Have you ever thought that one parent doesn't care about you? Is it hard to remember the good times you have had with each parent? Does it seem like one parent is all good and the other is all bad? This can happen to kids whose parents are getting divorced. You might start to believe that one of your parents isn't a safe and loving parent when it isn't true. If this happens, you have forgotten the truth. If you forget the truth, it is easy to be mad at a parent for the hurt you feel. Remembering the truth about each parent is one of the most important things you can do. That way you can love and feel loved by both parents.

Make Good Choices

Does one parent ask you to do things that may hurt or upset the other parent? Examples include spying on a parent, keeping a secret from a parent, or calling a stepparent "mom" or "dad." Do you agree to these things because you don't know what else to do? Do your choices cause problems in your relationship with one of your parents? Sometimes kids get confused about how to make good choices. They can hurt themselves or a parent when they don't mean to. If you think about your options and try to choose the best one for you, you will be making good choices. Then you will be able to love and feel loved by both parents.

Make Yourself Proud

Have you done or said things to a parent that don't feel right? When parents are divorcing, sometimes kids do things that make it hard for them to feel proud. They may be rude or hurtful to one parent just to make the other parent happy. If you know your values, such as honesty and kindness, you can live by them. Then you will be proud of yourself, and you will be able to love and feel loved by both parents.

Be Brave

Have you ever chosen to not do the right thing because it was hard? For example, have you found it hard to tell one parent that you don't want to hurt the other parent's feelings? Sometimes kids whose parents are getting divorced can be afraid to do the right thing. It can be hard to be brave. It can be hard to act in ways that don't hurt a parent. If you act with courage and are brave, you will feel better and make better choices, even when they are hard. Then you will be able to love and feel loved by both parents.

Keep Trying

Have you felt discouraged and thought that nothing will get better? Do you feel like your parents will always fight? Do you feel like giving up one parent just to please the other? If you can remember to say encouraging things to yourself, you will be able to keep trying to do the things you need to do so you can love and feel loved by both parents.

Get the Help You Need

Do you ever feel like you are dealing with your parents' problems all alone? Do you feel like you aren't getting enough help from other people? Sometimes kids whose parents are getting divorced need help dealing with their feelings. Sometimes they need a friend or a grown-up to help them figure out how to deal with their parents' problems. When you figure out who to ask for help, you can find the help you need. With help it will be easier to love and feel loved by both parents.

Take Care of Your Mind and Body

Is your parents' divorce and fighting making you feel tired or achy? Is it hard focusing and keeping your mind on school stuff? Sometimes kids whose parents are getting divorced carry a lot of stress in their mind and body. That doesn't feel good. If you can remember to de-stress, you will be able to take care of yourself and have the strength and energy you need to love and feel loved by both parents.

Being a kid with parents who are getting divorced can be tough! Sometimes it can be hard to follow the rules. That's why we are going to teach you different ways to follow them so you can love and feel loved by both parents. But first, you are going to think of a workbook buddy.

When Your Parents Fight

Activity 1: Think of a Workbook Buddy

Think of a workbook buddy who can be with you in your mind and heart as you go through this workbook. That way you won't have to go through it alone. Your buddy should be loyal and wise and help you feel safe even when you have strong feelings. Your buddy will help you find strength and courage when you need it.

Sit back and close your eyes. Who helps you feel calm and safe? Is it a person or an animal? In the space below, draw your buddy. Don't forget to give him or her a name.

We will remind you to think of your buddy as you go through the workbook. We will show you pictures of a friendly animal who will remind you that you are not alone. Your buddy is watching out for you!

Your buddy says, *"I am always here to help you. You are not alone. I will take this journey with you."*

Getting Through My Parents' Divorce

Activity 2: Things Parents Fight About

This workbook is about you and how you are dealing with your parents' divorce. Every family is the same in some ways and different in other ways. But most kids have a hard time when their parents fight. Divorcing parents can fight about a lot of different things.

Circle the things below that your parents fight about. Put a star next to the ones that bother you the most. You can use your answers as you go through the workbook.

What clothes you wear	What hobbies you have	What you eat
Time you spend with each parent	What music you listen to	Your chores
What movies you see	What your hair looks like	Your name
Where the pets live	What video games you play	Child support
Who your doctors are	Who your friends are	Holidays
Your homework	What school you go to	School vacations

A Workbook for Children Coping with Divorce, Parental Alienation, and Loyalty Conflicts

Feelings, Feelings, Feelings

Did you know that most kids have strong feelings when their parents fight? Strong feelings can be hard to manage until you know how to name them and cope with them. They can get in the way of following the rules for loving and feeling loved by both parents.

Activity 3: Feelings Kids Have When Parents Fight

Circle the feelings you think kids have when their parents don't get along. Put a star by the feelings you had this past week.

sad   angry   afraid   guilty

worried   confused   hurt

Did you circle and put a star next to all of the feelings? You probably did. That's because when parents fight, kids have all sorts of feelings.

It helps to name your feelings.

Did you know that naming a feeling can make you feel better? The next time you have a strong feeling, think about what you are feeling and give it a name. Try saying, "I am feeling _____ right now."

It is important to allow yourself to have feelings.

Did you know that accepting your feelings makes you feel better? By accepting them, you know it is okay to have them. Feelings are not right or wrong. You don't have to ignore them or push them away because they hurt. It can help to say out loud, "I accept all of my feelings. They are part of me." Try making up a little song to help you accept your feelings.

My feelings might be sad.

My feelings might be mad.

Sometimes it's hard

When I'm in between

Mom and Dad.

Feelings do not last forever!

When you have have a strong feeling, it may feel like the feeling will always be there. But feelings come and go. They don't last. The next time you have a strong feeling, try saying, "I am feeling _____ right now, but I will feel better and different soon."

Activity 4: Start a Feeling Journal

In a notebook or journal, write down what you are feeling. Choose a few times a day to write in your journal. It could be after breakfast, before dinner, or before bedtime. After you write in your journal for a few days you will probably see that your feelings change during the day and from day to day. Was it hard to be okay with any of your feelings? Did you think any of your feelings were good or bad?

You know that feelings don't last forever, and that it's okay to have them. But it doesn't feel good when you have a strong feeling, and it is okay to tell yourself that. You might say to yourself, *Gee, I am feeling kind of sad right now. I wish I weren't. I wouldn't want my friend to feel this way, but it's okay.*

Activity 5: Feelings About Divorce

Read the story and then answer the questions below.

Brandy and Justin are ten-year-old twins. They live with their mom and dad. Brandy and Justin are doing homework when their mom calls them into the living room. They think they did something wrong and quietly sit down on the couch, as their mother asks them to. Instead of getting scolded, she tells them that their dad is moving out of the home because they are getting a divorce. Brandy starts to cry.

"Doesn't Daddy love us anymore?" Brandy asks her mom.

"Of course he does, honey," Mom explains. "It is just that we have been fighting a lot. I think you know that because you hear us yelling. We want to have more peace in our lives, and we think we can have that if our family lives in two homes."

Justin feels like he is boiling inside. "You are both stupid," he calls out as he throws his book on the floor. He races to his bedroom and slams the door.

What are Brandy and Justin probably feeling when they go into the living room?

_____

What do you think it was like for Brandy and Justin to hear their parents yelling at each other?

_____

Do you think Brandy and Justin wish their parents would stay together even though they fight?

_____

Why does Brandy cry? _____

What is Justin feeling when he is "boiling" inside? _____

How are you like Brandy? _____

_____

How are you like Justin? _____

_____

Activity 6: Situations and Feelings

When parents are getting divorced, kids have strong feelings. It may help you to know that other kids, such as Brandy and Justin, have strong feelings as well. It can help to know what situations can lead to certain feelings. This way, when you expect a feeling to come, you may not feel as bothered by it.

Draw a line from the feeling to a situation that causes you to have that feeling. There are no right or wrong answers. You may have the same feeling in different situations. It's okay if one feeling has many lines coming to it or if one situation has many lines connected to it.

Mom and Dad yell at each other.

Worried

One parent says something private and personal about the other parent.

Sad   One parent puts down the rules of the other parent.

One parent says mean and untrue things about the other parent.

Angry

You ignore or are rude to one parent so the other parent will be nicer to you.

Confused   One parent hints that you should spend more time with him or her.

One parent tries to get you to move in with him or her.

Afraid

One parent calls the other parent by his or her first name.

Guilty   One parent gets rid of photos of the other parent.

One parent calls you a name and says you are just like the other parent.

Hurt

One parent says the other parent is trying to get all of the family's money.

Activity 7: Expressing Feelings

Kids have strong feelings when their parents don't get along. It is never wrong to have a feeling. But there are different ways kids deal with feelings. Some may be helpful and some may be unhelpful. If you follow the rules, it will be easier to love and feel loved by both parents. You deserve to be loved!

Draw a line from the feeling to a way to deal with the feeling that you think would be helpful. There are no right or wrong answers. It's okay if one feeling has many lines coming to it or if one way of dealing has many lines connected to it.

Worried

Talk to a friend who cares

Figure out what's bothering you

Talk to a counselor

Stay in bed

Sad

Cry

Accept the feeling

Do nothing

Angry

Watch a sad movie

Write in a journal

Draw a picture

Confused

Wish things could be better

Name the feeling

Afraid

Yell at someone

Talk to a parent

Hug a pet

Guilty

Do something really special for yourself

Have a temper tantrum

Hurt

Talk to yourself with kind words

Join a support group at school

When Your Parents Fight

Your buddy says, *"I will help you be okay with your feelings.
Together we'll find good ways to show them."*

Things to Remember

It's hard when parents have conflict.

Kids can have strong feelings.

You are not alone.

Your buddy can help you be okay with your feelings.

If you follow the rules, you will be able to love and feel loved by both parents.

Getting Through My Parents' Divorce

Thinking for Yourself

You Can Remember the Truth About Each Parent When You Think for Yourself

It is easy to be wrong when you don't have all the information!

What do you see?

A   13   C

Now what do you see?

12   13   14

Did you know that the middle figure is the same in both lines? In the first line it looks like the letter *B* because it is between letters. In the second line it looks like the number 13 because it is between numbers. Sometimes it's hard to see the truth.

It is easy to make mistakes when you are being misled!

Your buddy says, *"Everyone makes mistakes, and that's okay."*

Sometimes when parents fight they say things that aren't true about the other parent. Have you ever heard untrue things about a parent? If you believe something about a parent that is not true, it could create problems. For example, what if your dad told you that your mom said something mean about you, but she really didn't? You would be mad at your mom for no reason. That could hurt your relationship with your mom and keep you from enjoying your time with her. You wouldn't be following the rules for loving and feeling loved by both parents.

Or how about this? What if your parents decided together to get a divorce but you blame your dad because you think it was his choice? That could hurt your relationship with your dad. You are blaming him for something he didn't do. It could stop you from spending time with him or having fun when you do. You wouldn't be following the rules for loving and feeling loved by both parents.

It can be confusing when parents separate or divorce. It can be easy to make mistakes. After all, you're just a kid. But you can avoid mistakes when you think for yourself, change your mind if you made a mistake, and admit when you are wrong. When you think for yourself, you can avoid believing things about your parents that are not true. You will be able to follow the rules for loving and feeling loved by both parents.

Activity 8: Knowing Your Own Thoughts and Feelings

Think of something you believe. Is your teacher fair? Do you enjoy a hobby? Are the '49ers the best team ever? Or is Lady Gaga the greatest female singer? Fill in the blanks below about your idea.

I believe _____ .

	The idea is true	The idea is not true
Facts that show…		
Memories that show…		
Feelings I have that show…		
People who agree that…		
How I would feel if…		
People who would be mad if I believe…		

Now that I have thought for myself, I believe _____ .

Have fun thinking about other beliefs on a separate piece of paper. If you practice, you will get used to thinking for yourself. You will become an expert! This skill will help you later in the workbook when you test your beliefs about divorce.

Your buddy says, *"It's okay to change your mind. You are becoming an expert at thinking for yourself."*

Considering Your Options

You Can Make Good Choices When You Consider Your Options

Life is full of choices. Sometimes it is hard to know the right choice. Have you ever had a hard time making the right choice? Let's say a friend asks you to give him the answer to a math problem. You are not sure what you want to do, so you say okay so he will like you. Or maybe a parent asks you to keep a secret from the other parent. You are not sure what to do, so you agree to keep the secret so the one parent won't be angry with you. Sometimes it is hard to know which option will allow you to love and feel loved by both parents.

You may have a hard time seeing choices when feelings are strong or when you are afraid of upsetting somebody. Anger, fear, or worry can cause your mind and heart to race, and that gets in the way of seeing choices. Your mind becomes like a car stuck in the mud with all of its tires spinning. Another way to think about it is that feelings can freeze the brain. If that happens, you can use the STEP solution to unfreeze it. You will make better choices when your brain isn't frozen.

Unfreezing the Brain: The STEP Solution

The letters in STEP are to remind you what to do when you need more time to consider your options.

S   Step back and slow down

T   Take time

E   Explore options with brainstorming

P   Picture the solution and imagine putting it into practice

S: Step Back and Slow Down

The first step is slowing down. When someone asks you to do something that you may not want to do, remind yourself to *step* back and to *slow* down.

T: Take Time

Take time to think about your choices. Let the person know that you are not ready to make a choice. Here are some things you can say to show that you need more time:

"I need to think about that. I will get back to you."

"I am not sure. Let me think it over."

"I cannot make a decision right now. I need some time."

E: Explore Options

Explore and brainstorm options. Make a list of all the things you can do. Don't cross any ideas off your list, even silly or wild ones. For example, if a friend is pressuring you to help him cheat on a test, you might think, *Send him to the moon*. You can't actually do that. But you can take a break from the friendship if it doesn't feel right. You can also come up with other ideas, such as offering to tutor him or to study with him.

P: Picture and Practice in Your Mind

Picture the different options. Which one is the best one for you? Can you see yourself doing one option more easily than the rest? It might help you to practice an option in your mind before you actually do it.

Activity 9: Explore Options and Picture and Practice in Your Mind

Explore Options

Read the story below and then explore options. Explain why or why you don't like each option.

> David enjoys playing soccer. He is happy that both parents come to his game, even though they stand far away from each other. At halftime David's dad usually waves David over to where he is standing. David doesn't have time to visit with his mom. For a while David goes when he is called over, but then he realizes that there may be other options. What else could David do if he doesn't want to spend every halftime with his dad?

Ask to see a counselor to talk about the problem. _____

_____

Ask his coach for help. _____

_____

Tell his dad that he feels pressured when he waves him over. _____

_____

Stop playing soccer. _____

_____

Ask his mom to stop coming to the games. _____

_____

Tell his mom that he won't be able to speak to her at halftime. _____

_____

Do nothing. _____

_____

Picture and Practice in Your Mind

Which option can you picture yourself doing? _____

Why? _____

_____

When you pictured it in your mind, did it feel right? _____

(If you answered no, go back to the list and choose another option. Keep trying until you find one that you can picture yourself really doing.)

Practice Using STEP

Think of a problem that you want to use to explore options. Think of one that isn't about your parents' divorce. Remember, think of all options, no matter how silly, and write them on the lines below. Then picture and practice in your mind. Which options can you see yourself doing?

I want to brainstorm _____ .

Options:

1. _____

_____

2. _____

_____

3. _____

_____

4. _____

_____

5. _____

_____

Did any of the options—even a silly or wild one—lead you to a good solution? Which option can you see yourself doing?

_____

Your buddy says, *"You can choose any option you want, even a silly one, as long as it works for you!"*

Saying what you want can be hard!

Sometimes you can see the right option. The problem is that it is hard to tell the person what option you want. If a friend asks you to lie to your mom and dad and you don't want to, it might be hard to say no to that friend. Maybe you are afraid your friend will be mad at you. Maybe you don't want your friend to laugh at you. Maybe you are worried your friend will not like you anymore. There are a lot of reasons why it is hard to say what you want. Maybe it's hard to think of the right words to use.

There are lots of ways to say what you want!

Activity 10: Saying What You Want

What if a friend wants your pencil but you don't want to share it? In the list below check the boxes for the statements that you think might work in this situation.

☐ I need this pencil, but I can tell you where you can get one.

☐ I guess you can have it.

☐ I am using the pencil right now. Can you ask someone else?

☐ My parents said that I have to hold on to my school supplies. Sorry.

☐ Yes, but please give it back when you are done.

☐ I promised my sister that I would bring it home and let her use it.

☐ This is my lucky pencil. I don't want to lose it.

☐ I can loan you a pen, but I need this pencil.

☐ Why are you always asking me for things?

There are usually many polite and respectful ways to say what you want.

Your buddy says, *"What you want is important to me. Let it be important to you too."*

Living Your Values

You Feel Proud When You Live Your Values

People have a set of core values that helps define who they are. Values are what matters most to them. Examples of core values are honesty, kindness, intelligence, and creativity. Here's another way to think about a value. If you are given a choice to sign up for a sport or for band and you choose band, that might mean you value music over sports.

People feel good about themselves when their choices go with their values. But sometimes making choices that match your values is hard. Someone you love may tell you to think and feel something that you don't agree with. A parent may ask you to do something that goes against what you believe. You may do something that makes it hard for you to love and feel loved by both parents.

How Do You Know When You Haven't Been True to Your Values?

✔   You feel like you did something wrong.

✔   You feel guilty that you hurt someone.

✔   You feel bad about yourself.

✔   You feel confused about why you did something.

✔   People you care about are telling you that you are behaving "out of character."

✔   You feel like you don't know yourself.

✔   You feel like you are making choices for someone else, not for yourself.

✔   You are surprised by your actions.

✔   You do something that makes it hard to love and feel loved by both parents.

Knowing your core values will make it harder for someone to get you to act against your values. Any time you think, *I'm not sure this is right for me,* look at what you are doing and see if it goes against a core value.

Activity 11: Finding Your Core Values

Circle the core values that mean the most to you, whether you have them or just want to have them.

Working hard	Being smart	Being relaxed	Being clean
Being truthful	Being friendly	Being nice	Standing up for yourself
Being kind	Doing a good job	Being sure of yourself	Being fair
Being cool	Being helpful	Being popular	Being fun to be with
Being polite	Being artistic	Being curious	Being eager
Being cooperative	Being wise	Being respectful	Trying hard
Being a good friend	Getting good grades	Being considerate of your parents	

Activity 12: Knowing Your Core Values

Think of a character you like in a book. What qualities and beliefs does the character have that you admire?

_____

_____

_____

_____

Think of a character you like in a movie. What qualities and beliefs does the character have that you admire?

_____

_____

_____

_____

What are the qualities and beliefs you like most in your best friend?

_____

_____

_____

Think of a family member. What are the qualities and beliefs you like most in this person?

_____

_____

Are there common core values across these lists? Did you notice if certain ones keep coming up?

Finally, what qualities and beliefs of yours are you most proud of?

_____

_____

Your buddy says, *"Sometimes it's hard to live your values. But it is important to try."*

WOODSON

Activity 13: Living Your Core Values

Read the following statements and check the ones that would help you live your core values. If you want, you can write down the value for each action you check. There are no right or wrong answers.

☐ You and a parent keep a secret from the other parent. _____

☐ You follow the rules at each parent's home. _____

☐ You skip practice or miss a game because the parent you are staying with doesn't like that the other parent will be there. _____

☐ You are polite to both parents even when they are mad at each other. _____

☐ You tell one parent you don't want to keep secrets from the other parent. _____

☐ You don't spy on a parent when the other parent asks you to. _____

☐ You always tell the truth to both parents. _____

☐ You call a stepparent "Mom" or "Dad." _____

☐ You don't refer to your parents by their first names. _____

☐ When spending time with one parent you constantly text and call the other parent. _____

☐ You don't take sides when your parents disagree. _____

☐ You stick to the parenting schedule even when a parent tries to get you to change it. _____

☐ You start to think one parent is all good and the other is all bad. _____

Coping Tools

Your buddy says, *"You will feel good about yourself when you are true to your core values. Sometimes it takes courage."*

Acting with Courage

You Can Be Brave When You Act with Courage

When people are afraid to do things but do them anyway, they use courage. Did you know that you have courage inside of you? Think about it. Have you ever:

✔ Asked a question when you were scared?

✔ Said no when others wanted you to go against your values?

✔ Talked about scary things?

✔ Kept going when you felt like giving up?

✔ Admitted you were wrong?

✔ Tried new things that seemed weird or different?

Activity 14: You Were Courageous When...

Sometimes it is hard to remember that you have courage. To help you remember, you can think about times from the past when you found the courage you needed. Fill in the blanks for the situations that apply to you.

You were courageous when you told the truth about _____.

You were courageous when you helped a friend by _____

_____.

You were courageous when you helped a student with a disability by _____

_____.

You were courageous when you decided to _____
even though you were afraid.

You were courageous when you told a friend you wouldn't _____

_____.

You were courageous when you told your parents _____

_____.

Activity 15: Inspiring Courage Within Yourself

Sometimes people think about inspiring sayings to feel strong. That strength can help you love and feel loved by both parents. Here are some ways to help you find your courage.

- Find or create a courage quote. Use it as a bookmark so that every time you see it you are reminded of courage.

- Find a picture that reminds you of courage. Use it as wallpaper on your cell phone or computer.

- Find an inspiring song that gives you courage. Add it to your playlist and listen to it when you need courage.

- Find a charm that reminds you that you have courage inside. Carry it on a key chain, cell phone, camera, or necklace.

- Draw a picture of yourself being courageous. You can include your buddy in the picture if you want. Look at it when you need courage.

Your buddy says, *"I can see the courage inside of you!"*

Encouraging Yourself

You Keep Trying When You Encourage Yourself

Isn't it great when someone offers you encouragement! Did you know that you can encourage yourself? You can say positive and helpful things inside your head. All kids talk to themselves inside their heads. It is called *self-talk*.

Self-talk can be encouraging or discouraging.

A few words can make a big difference in how you feel. Let's say you want to learn basketball. You could say to yourself, *I am too short or I am too clumsy and I will never make the team*. With such negative self-talk, you probably won't even try out. But what if you say to yourself, *I may be short, but Nate Robinson was short and became a great player. At least I can try. It might be fun*. You will probably try out, and you might even make the team. You can see how self-talk can help or get in the way.

What can I say that would encourage me?

When you say good things to yourself, look up with your eyes. There's a part of your brain that works better when you look up. And by doing this, your self-talk will help you even more!

Activity 16: Is Your Self-Talk Helpful?

Below are some things you could say to yourself. If the statement would be helpful to you, label it *E* for "encouraging." If the statement would not be helpful to you, label it *D* for "discouraging."

_____ I am no good at this.

_____ My parents must not love me anymore.

_____ I have the courage to say or do what's right.

_____ It's all my fault.

_____ I've done this before and I can do it again.

_____ It feels good to be true to myself.

_____ I can't do this. It's too hard.

_____ I'll mess up. It's hopeless.

_____ I am good at this.

_____ I will never be happy living in two homes.

_____ It's my fault my parents are getting a divorce.

_____ This will be fun.

_____ I made a mistake, but I can do better next time.

_____ Wow! I really did great on that test.

_____ Things will get better.

_____ I can love and feel loved by both parents.

Self-talk affects how you feel and affects the choices you make. For example, if you tell yourself, *I made a mistake, but I can do better next time*, you might feel sad, but also hopeful. But if you said, *I made a mistake, and I'll never do better*, you might feel hopeless, worthless, or even guilty. Using self-talk that is encouraging will help you think clearer, see more options, stay true to your values, and act with courage.

Activity 17: Practicing Self-Talk

For each situation below, write helpful (encouraging) and not helpful (discouraging) self-talk along with the feelings you might have. Here is an example:

~~~~~~~~~~

Situation: Two friends are arguing.

Encouraging self-talk: They will work it out.   **Feeling:** relief

Discouraging self-talk: This is a disaster!   **Feeling:** fear

~~~~~~~~~~

Situation: Your dad makes fun of the rules at your mom's house.

Encouraging self-talk: _____ Feeling: _____

Discouraging self-talk: _____ Feeling: _____

~~~~~~~~~~

Situation: You want to try out for a sport.

Encouraging self-talk: _____ Feeling: _____

Discouraging self-talk: _____ Feeling: _____

~~~~~~

Situation: You wonder why you were not invited to a birthday party your best friend was invited to.

Encouraging self-talk: _____ Feeling: _____

Discouraging self-talk: _____ Feeling: _____

~~~~~~

Situation: Your parent asks you to do chores, but you have homework.

Encouraging self-talk: _____ Feeling: _____

Discouraging self-talk: _____ Feeling: _____

~~~~~~

Situation: You see a lost animal with a collar wandering around your neighborhood.

Encouraging self-talk: _____ Feeling: _____

Discouraging self-talk: _____ Feeling: _____

~~~~~~~~~~~~

Situation: Your parents' fighting is getting you down.

Encouraging self-talk: _____ Feeling: _____

Discouraging self-talk: _____ Feeling: _____

~~~~~~~~~~~~

Situation: One parent asks you to do something that might hurt the other parent's feelings.

Encouraging self-talk: _____ Feeling: _____

Discouraging self-talk: _____ Feeling: _____

Your buddy reminds you, *"Listen to your self-talk and make sure it's encouraging!"*

De-stressing Your Mind and Body

You Can Take Care of Your Mind and Body When You De-stress

Strong feelings can be stressful. You may feel stress in different parts of your body. Stress can be a racing heart, a stomachache, a headache, or tiredness.

What is happening in your body when you feel stress? In the animal world, when a big animal chases a smaller animal, the animal being chased feels stress. Its heart beats faster and it breathes faster. Stress helps the smaller animal run faster so it can get away from the bigger animal. Stress can be helpful. In the kid world, the same thing happens. When Mom and Dad fight with each other, you might feel stress. Your heart beats faster and you breathe faster. You probably aren't really in danger with Mom and Dad, but it can feel like you are. The stress helps you know what to do to help yourself and gives you the energy to do it.

Your buddy says, *"If you or someone in your family is getting hurt, or you feel unsafe, call 911 or run to a neighbor's house."*

Activity 18: What Ways Do You Feel Stress?

There are lots of ways to feel stress in your body. Check the boxes next to the ways you have felt stress, or add your own.

☐ Shortness of breath

☐ Tension in shoulders

☐ Sweaty palms

☐ Hungry

☐ Butterflies in the stomach

☐ Headache

☐ Jittery

☐ Racing heart

☐ Tired all over

☐ Other _____

☐ Other _____

☐ Other _____

Activity 19: Where Do You Feel Stress in Your Body When Your Parents Fight?

On the lines below, write where you feel stress when your parents fight.

You hear your parents fighting about your grades, your activities, or who pays for your school clothes. You might feel stress in your _____.

One parent wants you to be with him or her when you are supposed to be with the other parent. You might feel stress in your _____.

One parent won't let you have your cell phone, clothes, or computer at the other parent's home. You might feel stress in your _____.

One parent says the rules at the other parent's house are silly and that you don't need to follow them. You might feel stress in your _____.

One parent is really mad and wants you to testify against the other parent in court. You might feel stress in your _____.

Your parents get in a fight in front of your friends. You might feel stress in your _____.

One parent is talking about moving to another town and wants to take you. You might feel stress in your _____.

One parent is very sad when you are at the other parent's house. You might feel stress in your _____.

Activity 20: Letting Go of Stress

Stress doesn't feel good. If you can let go of stress, you will have more energy, you will think clearer, and you will feel better. By letting go of it, you will be able to follow the rules for loving and feeling loved by both parents. Here is one idea to help you let go of stress. The more you practice it, the easier it will be. You don't always have to do the whole activity. Sometimes you may only want to work on the part of your body that is feeling stress, and just repeat the activity several times.

Think of a safe place. If you can go there, take this workbook with you. If you can't go there, think about your safe place. See it in your mind. Imagine that you are there and feel how good it is to be safe. If it helps you to feel safe, have your buddy there with you.

Sit or lie down. Take a deep breath. Make sure you are comfortable. Close your eyes if you want, or just look at something until your eyes get tired and want to close on their own.

Think about your body. Notice how you are breathing. Take another deep breath. Pay attention to one part of your body at a time. Start with your shoulders. Do you feel tension in your shoulders? If so, take your breath in through your nose, and as you breathe out through your mouth imagine the tension and stress flowing out of your shoulders and leaving your body. It may help to raise and lower your shoulders as you breathe.

Now think of your chest. Does it feel tight and tense? If so, take your breath in slowly through your nose. Now imagine the tension escaping your body in your breath as you breathe out through your mouth.

Now move on to your arms and hands. Are your hands balled up into fists? Do your arms feel tense? If so, take your breath in through your nose. Now imagine all of the tension leaving your arms and hands as you breathe out through your mouth. Spread your fingers apart. Pay attention to each finger on each hand as the tension leaves your body.

Go through all the parts of your body this way. When you find tension, breathe in slowly and deeply through your nose and out through your mouth.

Let go of tightness and worries as you breathe out. You will feel more relaxed and calm with each breath.

If it helps, you can imagine that you are giving your stress to your buddy to hold.

Your buddy says, *"I will hold your stress for you so you can feel relaxed and calm."*

Activity 21: More Ways to Let Go of Stress

There are lots of ways to relieve stress!

In the chart shown are some quick activities to help you relieve stress. Check the box that describes how you feel each one works for you.

Coping Tools

	Never tried it	Tried it and it works okay	Tried it and it works well	Plan to try it soon
Jumping jacks, push-ups, jogging, other exercise				
Drawing, doodling				
Talking with a friend				
Writing in a journal				
Crying				
Sleeping				
Eating				
Deep breathing, yoga				
Reading				
Dancing, gymnastics				
Video games				
Arts and crafts				
Schoolwork				
Karate, tai kwan do, other martial arts				
Listening to music, playing an instrument				
Team sports such as soccer, baseball, basketball				
Talking with a caring adult or counselor				
Surfing the Internet				
Working on a puzzle or other challenging task				
Other				
Other				

Asking for Help from Others

You Can Get the Help You Need When You Ask Others for Help

Sometimes people can deal with their feelings and problems with courage and self-talk. Sometimes feelings and problems are so big they need to be shared with another person. Talking things out with others can make feelings and problems seem smaller and less scary. If you share them, you might think more clearly and find solutions more easily. How do you know when you need to ask for help?

✔ You are puzzled.

✔ You feel confused.

✔ You want to share your thoughts and feelings.

✔ You have strong feelings of sadness, anger, worry, fear, guilt, confusion, or hurt that stay with you for more than a day or two.

✔ You have tried other ways to help yourself and still feel the same.

✔ You want advice.

✔ You think you would feel better if you asked for help.

✔ You have conversations in your head in which you share your thoughts and feelings.

Other people can help you deal with your feelings and problems!

Feeling	Asking others for help can...
Worried	Help you find ways to be calmer and less stressed.
Sad	Help you feel less sad because you feel understood and cared for.
Angry	Help you figure out how to let go of your anger.
Confused	Help you figure out what is bothering you.
Afraid	Help you figure out if you have something to be afraid of.
Hurt	Help you feel cared about and understood.
Guilty	Help you figure out if you really did something wrong.

Asking others for help can allow you to practice all of your coping tools!

Coping tool	Asking others for help can...
Thinking for yourself	Help you figure out what you believe, why you believe it, and what would happen if you changed your mind.
Considering your options	Help you brainstorm options and find the one right for you.
Living your values	Help you identify your core values and determine how to use them to make good choices.
Acting with courage	Help you remember your courage in the past so you can act with courage in the future.
Encouraging yourself	Help you stay positive with self-talk.
De-stressing	Help you figure out how to relax and take care of yourself.

There are all sorts of people whom you can ask for help and support!

Activity 22: Helpful Qualities

Whom could you ask for help? What kind of person do you want to ask? There are all sorts of people who want to support you! Unscramble the words for ideas of the kind of person you want for support. (Your buddy has the answers on page 50.)

1. easf

2. plfehul

3. siew

4. idnk

5. gcianr

6. tesnoh

7. doog letsinre

8. arfi

9. caml

10. alylo

11. wuosrrtthty

Activity 23: Who Would You Ask for Help?

Who from the list below would you ask for help? There are no right or wrong answers. Check as many or as few boxes as you want.

☐ Someone who is trustworthy and won't tell others what you shared.

☐ Someone who has gone through the same thing you are going through.

☐ Someone who is an adult.

☐ Someone who laughs at you.

☐ Someone who is a tried-and-true friend.

☐ Someone you know from school.

☐ Someone you just met.

☐ Someone who hurt your best friend.

☐ Someone your parents know.

☐ Someone who won't make fun of you, no matter what you say.

☐ Someone who will help you problem solve and find answers.

☐ Someone who will listen and won't tell you what to do.

☐ Someone who is kind.

☐ Someone who borrowed something and didn't return it.

☐ Someone who seems to have good suggestions and ideas.

☐ Someone who won't take either of your parent's side and will only think about what is right for you.

Activity 24: Finding Helpful People

Who can you reach out to when you feel like you are in the middle of a parent problem? Look at the list below. Check the box next to the people who you feel like you could talk to. Write the person's name and how you would contact him or her. In the first example, write the teacher's name on the first line. On the second line write something like, "After school on a Wednesday when the teacher is there late in the day."

☐ A teacher at school: _____

_____

☐ A coach: _____

_____

☐ A parent of a friend: _____

_____

☐ A friend: _____

_____

☐ A religious teacher: _____

_____

☐ A school counselor: _____

_____

☐ A therapist: _____

_____

☐ A grandparent: _____

_____

☐ A brother or sister: _____

_____

☐ An aunt, uncle, or other relative: _____

_____

☐ A peer counselor from school: _____

_____

☐ Other: _____

_____

Sometimes it's hard to ask for help!

You may wish to talk things over with another person but feel shy about asking. Are you worried the person won't understand you? Are you afraid the person won't have time for you? Are you embarrassed to share your thoughts and feelings? Asking for help is a skill you can practice. It will get easier the more you do it. Here are some suggestions.

- Write a letter or e-mail to the person. Ask if you can talk about something that is bothering you.

- Find a time when you think the person will be alone and ask if you can problem solve together.

- Write down your thoughts before asking for help. That way you will remember what you want to say if you get nervous.

- Use helpful self-talk to remind yourself that you can ask for the support you need.

- Draw on your courage to ask for help.

- Practice asking for help when you are by yourself. If you want to make an appointment with the school counselor but feel shy about doing it, here's what you could do: when you are alone in your room say out loud, "I would like to make an appointment with you, Mrs. Smith. How do I do that?"

Which of these suggestions do you think you will use? _____

Your buddy says, *"I am here for you, and so are lots of other people."*

(Answers to activity 22: 1. safe, 2. helpful, 3. wise, 4. kind, 5. caring, 6. honest, 7. good listener, 8. fair, 9. calm, 10. loyal, 11. trustworthy)

Things to Remember

Think for yourself so you remember the truth about your parents.

Live your core values so you feel proud.

Draw on your courage to do things you are afraid to do.

Use helpful self-talk to build confidence.

Use STEP to find the right choice.

Find the right people to ask for help.

Follow the rules for loving and feeling loved by both parents.

Getting Started

Kids face a lot of situations that are hard to handle when their parents are getting divorced. The coping tools we talked about in part 2 can help you deal with strong feelings that come up in these situations. The tools help you figure out what you believe and how you want to handle the feelings.

Activity 25: Which Situations Are Yours?

Which situations below seem familiar? Check the ones that cause strong feelings in you. These are the situations you want to think about as you go through the workbook.

☐   1.   One parent looks sad, angry, or hurt when you spend time with the other parent.

☐   2.   One parent asks you to spy on the other parent.

☐   3.   One parent says mean and untrue things about the other parent.

☐   4.   One parent allows you to choose whether or not to spend time with the other parent.

☐   5.   One parent doesn't want you to have pictures of the other parent.

☐   6.   One parent refers to the other parent by a first name rather than as "Mom" or "Dad."

☐   7.   One parent suggests you move in with him or her.

☐   8.   One parent ignores or puts down the rules and authority of the other parent.

☐   9.   One parent tells you that the other parent is dangerous.

☐   10.   One parent calls a stepparent "Mom" or "Dad" and suggests you do the same.

☐ 11. One parent tells you that the other parent doesn't love you anymore.

☐ 12. One parent interferes with your communication with the other parent.

☐ 13. One parent asks you to keep secrets from the other parent.

☐ 14. One parent doesn't include the other parent's contact information on school and athletic forms.

☐ 15. One parent gets annoyed or angry if you pay attention to the other parent.

☐ 16. One parent changes your last name to exclude the other parent.

☐ 17. One parent tells you private and personal information about the other parent.

☐ 18. One parent wants you to tell a custody evaluator, therapist, or judge that you don't like the other parent.

Using the Coping Tools

How Are You Feeling?

If you are dealing with situations like the ones you checked in activity 25, you may have lots of strong feelings. You may be stressed and upset. In part 3 you are going to learn how to use your coping tools to deal with your feelings. Coping with your feelings will help you love and feel loved by both parents.

You may need to take breaks from working on your feelings. It's hard work. So make a go-to list of things that you like doing. They should be things that make you feel good. If you make your list now, it will be ready for you when you need to take a break!

My Go-To List: Things That Make Me Feel Good

1. _____

2. _____

3. _____

4. _____

5. _____

When you are ready to start working on your feelings, choose a feeling from the following pages. As you work on these hard-to-handle feelings, keep in mind that you also have good feelings. Remember that life brings us happiness, joy, pleasure, and many other wonderful feelings too.

Sadness

What Is Sadness?

Sadness is a feeling that you get when you are unhappy. You might feel sad when you lose something you love or when things don't go the way you want them to.

Many kids feel sad when their parents get divorced. You might feel sad that your parents are fighting. You might feel sad that one parent is moving out of the house. You might feel sad that you have to leave your friends behind because one parent is moving to a new town. You might feel sad if one parent has done or said something to hurt the other parent.

How Is Sadness Helpful?

Sadness can be helpful. It shows you that there is something you want to feel better about. That's why it is good to deal with your sadness. When you do, you will feel happier, have more energy, enjoy yourself more, and be friendlier. You will be more able to follow the rules for loving and feeling loved by both parents.

How Is Sadness a Problem?

Sadness does not feel good in your body. It can stop you from doing things you enjoy, such as playing with friends. You may cry or feel like crying but don't know why. Too much sadness can cause you problems. Your brain can get tired, and you may not want to do schoolwork or other things you need to do. When kids feel sad about their parents' divorce, sometimes they end up feeling like they have to choose sides or the sadness won't go away. It can be hard to love and feel loved by both parents when you have strong sad feelings.

Reasons for Your Sadness: Real or Not Real?

Did you know that sad feelings can come from reasons that are real and reasons that are not real? Even though your feeling of sadness is real, the reasons for it may not be. You can see if the reasons for the sadness are real or not by thinking for yourself. If you find that the reasons are not real, your body and muscles may relax, and your sad feelings will probably leave. You may still have choices to make to deal with the situation, and you can use the coping tools to help you with that. If you find that the reasons behind your sadness are real, you can use your coping tools to make an action plan.

Let's say that you feel sad about getting a bad grade on a test because you spent time on the phone with a friend when you should have been studying. Should you be sad? After thinking for yourself you realize that the test grade did not count and no one got a good grade. There is no reason for the sadness. But you still decide to limit calls with that friend when you have your next test.

Suppose the test grade does count. The reason for the sadness is real. You realize you should have studied more. You usually do well on tests. You are getting upset and wondering what to do. Now it is time for an action plan. You consider your options and decide you need to talk to the teacher about why you got the bad grade. You use encouraging self-talk to help you feel brave and to remind yourself that you value learning. You go in to see the teacher when you know she will be alone. She reminds you that you were absent the day the class went over the study questions and that you really weren't ready for the test. She goes over the study questions with you and says that you can take a makeup test the next day. Dealing with the sadness helped you make a sad situation better.

Activity 26: What Does Sadness Feel Like?

What does sadness feel like in your mind and body? Circle the words below that describe how you feel when you are sad.

blah	no energy	cranky	stomachache
depressed	lonely	blue	not happy
tired	yearning	down	
gloomy	crying	headache	

Has anyone ever told you that you look sad?   _____ yes   _____ no

If yes, write down how that person could tell. _____

_____

_____

(Hint: Look in the mirror the next time you feel sad and write down what you see.)

Using Coping Tools to Deal with Sadness

The coping tools from part 2 can help you deal with sadness. Here's how. Imagine you are dealing with situation number 11 in activity 25 (on page 52). Let's say that your dad moves out because your parents are getting a divorce. Your mom tells you that your dad doesn't love you anymore, because if he did the family would still be together. She says that you don't have to spend time with him anymore because he doesn't really love you. When you hear that your dad doesn't love you, you feel really sad.

Coping tool	Example
Think for yourself: decide whether the cause of your sadness is real.	You remember all the good times you have had with your dad. You remember that he has called you every day to tell you what you will be doing when you spend time together. He tells you that you are important and loved. You remember that your dad will be taking you shopping to set up a room at his new house. You decide that he still loves you. You know your own truth about how much your parents love you.
Consider your options: use STEP to see your choices.	After using STEP, you remember that your parents love you even though they are getting divorced. You decide to make good choices. You tell your mom that you know your dad still loves you and that you want to spend time with both parents.
Live your values: be clear about what you will and will not do.	You think about your core value honesty. You decide to make yourself proud by telling your mom that you know your dad still loves you.
Act with courage: remember that you can be brave and do what is right.	Your mom wants you to say that you don't need to spend time with your dad anymore because he moved out. You feel sad when you think about saying something that isn't true. You find courage quotes that inspire you to be brave and to say what you know is true, which is that you love both of your parents and want to spend time with each of them.

Encourage yourself: remind yourself that you can be okay with your sadness.	You decide to use helpful self-talk, telling yourself, *I know both of my parents love me.*
De-stress: relax and take care of your mind and body.	You feel a lot of tension in your body, so you decide to play with your pet, which usually calms you down and makes you feel good.
Ask for help from others: find people who can help you cope with your sadness.	You decide to ask for help to deal with the sadness you feel. You talk to your coach. He shares with you that his parents fought a lot, too. His mom was the one who moved out, but that didn't mean she didn't love him anymore. He suggests ways for you to handle your sadness, and you feel better having shared your problem.

Your buddy says, *"I will help you with your sadness so it doesn't get too strong. You don't have to be alone with it."*

Sadness Action Plan: The Three Ds

Step 1: *Describe* your sadness and the reason for it. (Look at activity 25 to remind yourself of some of the situations that might cause you to feel sad.)

_____

_____

_____

_____

_____

_____

Step 2: *Decide* if the reason for your sadness is real by thinking for yourself.

	The idea is true	The idea is not true
Facts that show…		
Memories that show…		
Feelings I have that show…		
People who agree that…		
How I would feel if…		
People who would be mad if I believe…		

Circle your answer:

When I think for myself about the reason for my sadness, I realize that it is/is not real.

Step 3: *Dive* into your coping tools to help you with the situation.

Coping tool	What you have learned and what you plan to do
Consider your options: use STEP to see your choices	I choose this option:
Live your values	My core values that will help me are:
Act with courage	I will remind myself that I have courage by:
Encourage yourself	I will encourage myself by:
De-stress	I will de-stress by:
Ask for help from others	People who can help me are:

Your buddy says, *"You feel best when you deal with sadness. Coping with feelings helps you follow the rules for loving and feeling loved by both parents!"*

Worry

What Is Worry?

Worry is a feeling you can get when you are upset or bothered by something that may or may not happen. Kids often worry when they think about parent problems. You might worry that something bad is going to happen to the family because of divorce, or that one parent will ask you to do something you are not sure is right. You might worry about doing or saying the wrong thing. Sometimes kids worry that they might have to choose sides because their parents are getting divorced. Worrying makes it hard to love and feel loved by both parents.

How Is Worry Helpful?

Worry is a sign that you are uneasy or uncomfortable with something and need to make a change. It is a good idea to deal with worry. When you do, you will take care of what's bothering you. Then you'll have energy to enjoy yourself more. You will feel happier and be friendlier. If you deal with your worry, it will be easier to follow the rules for loving and feeling loved by both parents.

How Is Worry a Problem?

Worry doesn't feel good in your body. Too much of it can make it hard to focus or think about anything else. When you worry too much, your brain isn't free to do its best work. Let's say you have a big test coming up. You are worried about how you will do. You were absent when the teacher went over the study questions. You feel uneasy. Instead of studying you worry so much that your brain can't work.

Reasons for Your Worry: Real or Not Real?

Did you know that worry can be real or not real? Even though your feeling of worry is real, the reasons for it may not be. You can see if the reasons are real or not by thinking for yourself. If you find that the reasons are not real, you can relax, and use self-talk to encourage yourself to stop worrying. If the reasons behind your worry are real, use your coping tools to make an action plan.

Let's say you are worried that a friend is mad at you, and you can't sleep. Should you be worried? After thinking for yourself you realize how much your friend likes you, how you have worked things out in the past, and how much fun you have together. There is no reason for the worry. Now you know you don't need to worry, so you can relax and have a good night's sleep. You will be rested and ready to talk to your friend tomorrow!

But what if after thinking for yourself you realize that you should be worried? You said something about your friend that is not true. You have never done this before and don't know if your friend can forgive you. You don't feel ready to talk with your friend about it. Now it is time for an action plan. You consider your options and decide that you need to get help from your school counselor. You use encouraging self-talk to feel brave. You remember that you value loyalty, honesty, and friendship. Then you work out a plan with your counselor for how to talk with your friend.

Activity 27: What Does Worry Feel Like?

What does worry feel like in your mind and body? Circle the words below that describe how you feel when you are worried.

uneasy	jumpy	fidgety	bothered
joyful	happy	relaxed	peaceful
tense	trouble concentrating	upset	calm
anxious		bugged	

Has anyone ever told you that you look worried? _____ yes _____ no

If yes, write down how that person could tell. _____

_____

_____

(Hint: Look in the mirror the next time you feel worried and write down what you see.)

Using Coping Tools to Deal with Worry

The coping tools from part 2 can help you deal with your worry. Here's how. Imagine you are dealing with situation number 18 from activity 25. Your parents are going back to court and you are worried because you don't know what is going on. You ask your mother to tell you what is happening. She tells you not to worry, because you're just a kid and the grown-ups will handle the situation. But your dad tells you that you are such a mature and big kid that you deserve to know the truth. He shows you some court papers and says that you will be speaking to a doctor soon. When you do, you should tell the doctor the truth about your mom. Now you are really worried! What if he expects you to tell the doctor that you hate your mom?

Coping tools	Example
Think for yourself: decide whether the cause of your worry is real.	You think for yourself and realize that you don't hate either parent. In fact, you love them both very much.
Consider your options: use STEP to see your choices.	After using STEP you decide that you are not going to say something that isn't true. You hope that your dad can accept this. You decide to write it in a letter and hand it to him on Saturday morning at breakfast.
Live your values: be clear about what you will and will not do.	Your core value of honesty is really important to you, so you decide you won't say anything to the doctor that isn't true.
Act with courage: remember that you can be brave and do what is right.	You are worried about how your dad will handle you telling him that you still love your mom. You plan on talking to the doctor about this. You go online and find courage quotes to inspire you.
Encourage yourself: remind yourself that you can be okay with your worry.	You are worried that your dad will be mad at you for not wanting to tell the doctor that you hate your mom. You decide to use helpful self-talk, telling yourself, *I can handle it, no matter what happens.*

De-stress: relax and take care of your mind and body.	You are worried that your dad will be mad at you, so you feel a lot of tension in your body. You jog around the block while listening to your favorite music. Later you work on a jigsaw puzzle to take your mind off your parents.
Ask for help from others: find people who can help you cope with your worry.	You are worried that your parents will never stop fighting. You tell your friend that it's getting you down. He tells you about a group at school for kids whose parents are getting divorced. He finds it helpful. You decide to join the group so you can share your worries with others. You begin to feel better.

Your buddy says, *"I will help you with your worrying so you can feel calm. You don't have to be alone with it."*

Worry Action Plan: The Three Ds

Step 1: *Describe* your worry and the reason for it. (Look at activity 25 to remind yourself of situations that might cause you to worry.)

_____

_____

_____

_____

_____

_____

_____

Step 2: *Decide* if the reason for your worry is real by thinking for yourself.

	The idea is true	The idea is not true
Facts that show…		
Memories that show…		
Feelings I have that show…		
People who agree that…		
How I would feel if…		
People who would be mad if I believe…		

Circle your answer:

When I think for myself about the reason for my worry, I realize that it is/is not real.

Using the Coping Tools

Step 3: *Dive* into your coping tools to help you with the situation.

Coping tool	What you have learned and what you plan to do
Consider your options: use STEP to see your choices	I choose this option:
Live your values	My core values that will help me are:
Act with courage	I will remind myself that I have courage by:
Encourage yourself	I will encourage myself by:
De-stress	I will de-stress by:
Ask for help from others	People who can help me are:

Your buddy says, *"I will help you take care of your worry so you can feel your best. Coping with worry makes it easier to follow the rules for loving and feeling loved by both parents!"*

Anger

What Is Anger?

Anger is a feeling you get when you think someone has taken something from you or treated you wrongly or unfairly. It's hard to ignore anger. It is usually a strong emotion that quickly gets your attention. You might feel anger when your parents fight. You might feel anger when you think one of your parents doesn't love you. Sometimes kids get angry just because things are the way they are.

How Is Anger Helpful?

Anger can make you feel strong and powerful. It can give you energy when you need to make a change or make wrong things right. Anger can keep you working on a problem until you figure it out, sort of the way a car uses gas to drive down the road.

When Is Anger a Problem?

Sometimes anger is so strong that you might find it hard to manage. You may act in ways that are not good for you and do things you regret, such as being mean to other kids or breaking things. Some kids don't like to be around angry kids because angry kids can be scary. It can be a lot of work to deal with anger. Anger makes it hard to have fun and think clearly. Anger can make it hard to love and feel loved by both parents. Some kids even think they have to choose sides to stop the angry feelings.

Reasons for Your Anger: Real or Not Real?

Did you know that angry feelings can come from reasons that are real and reasons that are not real? Even though your feeling of anger is real, the reasons for it may not be. You can see if the reasons for the anger are real or not by thinking for yourself. If you find that the reasons are not real, your body and muscles may relax and your angry feelings will probably go away. If you find that the reasons behind your anger are real, you can use your coping tools to make an action plan.

Let's say that you feel angry because you think a friend said something mean about you to another friend. You decide to get back at the friend by not inviting her to your birthday party. She finds out and is really hurt and angry with you, especially because she never said anything bad about you in the first place. She tells you this. After thinking for yourself you realize that the anger made it hard for you to think clearly. You realize that you should have talked things over with your friend before assuming a rumor was true.

However, if you feel angry because your friend *did* say something mean about you, you can still use your coping tools to work out the problem with her.

Activity 28: What Does Anger Feel Like?

Rearrange the words in the sentences below to see where you might feel anger in your mind and body. (Your buddy has the answers on page 75.)

1. My adeh _____ is pounding and aches.

1. My feac _____ is warm and red.

1. My anhd _____ is balled into a fist. I might hit someone.

1. My thaer _____ is beating fast in my chest.

1. It is hard to breathe in my nulgs _____.

1. My rmas _____ are crossed in front of my chest.

1. I can't eat. I have a notk _____ in my stomach.

1. It's hard to run. My whole byod _____ feels tense.

Has anyone ever told you that you look angry?   _____ yes   _____ no

If yes, write down how that person could tell. _____

_____

_____

(Hint: Look in the mirror the next time you are angry and write down what you see.)

Using Coping Tools to Deal with Anger

The coping tools from part 2 can help you deal with anger. Here's how. Imagine you are dealing with situation number 8 from activity 25. Let's say your dad is upset that you didn't study for a test. He punishes you by taking away your cell phone for the weekend. Your mom tells you that the punishment is "ridiculous" and "crazy" and buys you a new cell phone. She tells you that you don't need to follow those crazy rules. Now you are angry with your dad for punishing you.

Coping tools	Example
Think for yourself: decide whether the cause of your anger is real.	You remember that your dad really loves you and wants you to do well in school. Parents have a responsibility to reward and punish their children, and that doesn't make them mean and crazy. You know that many of your friends have been punished in the same way, or worse, by their parents. You think that you should follow the rules at each parent's home, even if you don't like those rules.
Consider your options: use STEP to see your choices.	After using STEP you decide that you don't want to take the new cell phone. You realize that you will feel better if you follow the punishment, even if you don't like it. You find that you feel angry with your mom for trying to make you believe that your dad is wrong or crazy.
Live your values: be clear about what you will and will not do.	You value respect for authority and decide not to take the new phone, even though it looks pretty cool.
Act with courage: remember that you can be brave and do what is right.	You are nervous about telling your mom that you don't want the phone. You think about other brave people who resisted temptation and decide that you can do the same.

Encourage yourself: remind yourself that you can be okay with your anger.	You feel discouraged that your parents don't agree about family rules and punishment. But then you remind yourself that they don't have to agree. You can follow the rules at each parent's home. You decide that you will be okay no matter what happens.
De-stress: relax and take care of your mind and body.	When you think about your mom calling your dad's rules "crazy" and "ridiculous," you feel stress all over your body, especially in your stomach. You practice taking three deep breaths, like you learned in school. That really helps you relax.
Ask for help from others: find people who can help you cope with your anger.	You find a grown-up who can explain to your mom that it makes you angry when she tells you that your dad's rules are "ridiculous" and "crazy."

Your buddy says, *"Anger doesn't feel good, but you can handle it. I will help you with your anger so you don't have to feel alone with it."*

(Answers to activity 28: 1. head, 2. face, 3. hand, 4. heart, 5. lungs, 6. arms, 7. knot, 8. body)

Anger Action Plan: The Three Ds

Step 1: *Describe* your anger and the reason for it. (Look at activity 25 to remind yourself of some of the situations that might cause you to feel angry.)

_____

_____

_____

_____

_____

_____

Step 2: *Decide* if the reason for your anger is real by thinking for yourself.

	The idea is true	The idea is not true
Facts that show…		
Memories that show…		
Feelings I have that show…		
People who agree that…		
How I would feel if…		
People who would be mad if I believe…		

Circle your answer:

When I think for myself about the reason for my anger, I realize that it is/is not real.

Step 3: *Dive* into your coping tools to help you with the situation.

Coping tool	What you have learned and what you plan to do
Consider your options: use STEP to see your choices	I choose this option:
Live your values	My core values that will help me are:
Act with courage	I will remind myself that I have courage by:
Encourage yourself	I will encourage myself by:
De-stress	I will de-stress by:
Ask for help from others	People who can help me are:

Your buddy says, *"When you aren't so angry, it's easier to follow the rules for loving and feeling loved by both parents!"*

Hurt

What Is Hurt?

Hurt is a painful feeling. Some kids say they are brokenhearted because it feels so bad. You might feel hurt if one parent says that the other parent never wanted you or doesn't love you. You might feel hurt if a parent asks you to call a stepparent "Mom" or "Dad" and tells you it's because the stepparent does more for you than your other parent.

How Is Hurt Helpful?

Hurt lets you know that you feel let down by someone or something. It tells you that your world is not quite right. Hurt is like a STOP sign telling you to look around before you move ahead. You need to know what is hurting you in order to follow the rules for loving and feeling loved by both parents.

When Is Hurt a Problem?

Hurt takes energy away from you, making it hard to figure things out. It can make you feel weak. Hurt can make you doubt yourself. If you hurt for too long, you might start believing that you are bad. Hurt can make you want to run away and hide. Hurt can make it hard to love and feel loved by both parents. Some kids even believe they have to choose one parent over the other because hurt makes them feel powerless.

Reasons for Your Hurt: Real or Not Real?

Did you know that hurt feelings can come from reasons that are real and reasons that are not real? Even though your feeling of hurt is real, the reasons for it may not be. You can see if the reasons for the hurt feeling are real or not by thinking for yourself. If you find that the reasons are not real, your body and muscles may relax and your hurt feeling will probably go away. If you find that the reasons behind your hurt are real, you can use your coping tools to make an action plan.

Let's say that you feel hurt because you think a group of your friends are planning to get together without you. You see them whispering together, and you feel left out. It is time for an action plan. You consider your options and decide that you need to ask your friends what is going on. You use encouraging self-talk to feel brave and to remind yourself that you value friendship. If you find out that they are actually planning a surprise party for you, you won't be hurt anymore. The reason for the hurt you felt isn't real.

But if you find out that they really are excluding you from a get-together, the reason for the hurt is real. Now you can use your coping tools to figure out what is going on with your friendships and what you can do to make them better.

Activity 29: What Does Hurt Feel Like?

What does hurt feel like in your body? Most kids say they feel hurt in their stomachs and hearts. On the person below, choose a color or colors and draw what your hurt feels like. It can be any shape or color. Your hurt doesn't have to be in the stomach or heart.

Has anyone ever told you that you look hurt?   _____ yes   _____ no

If yes, write down how that person could tell. _____

_____

_____

(Hint: Look in the mirror the next time you feel hurt and write down what you see.)

Using Coping Tools to Deal with Hurt

The coping tools from part 2 can help you deal with your hurt. Here's how. Imagine you are dealing with situation number 4 in activity 25. Let's say your parents are fighting about where you are going to live. Your dad tells you that your mom only wants custody to get more child support, not because she really loves you and wants to spend more time with you. Your dad tells you that your mom doesn't really love you.

Coping tools	Example
Think for yourself: decide whether the cause of your hurt is real.	You remember all the times that your mom has done loving things for you. She does have a new family, but she still spends lots of time with you.
Consider your options: use STEP to see your choices.	After using STEP you decide that you don't believe your mom only wants custody to get money. She has shown you a lot of love. You realize that you feel upset at your dad for telling you that your mom doesn't love you.
Live your values: be clear about what you will and will not do.	You value truth, so you decide to tell your dad that you know your mom does love you.
Act with courage: remember that you can be brave and do what is right.	You are nervous about telling your dad that you believe your mom really does love you. You listen to your favorite song about being strong and decide that you can do the right thing.
Encourage yourself: remind yourself that you can be okay with your hurt.	You feel discouraged when you try to figure out why your dad would tell you that your mom doesn't love you. You know it isn't true. You decide that you don't have to figure out why your parents do what they do. That is grown-up stuff, and you can stay out of it. You decide that you will love both parents.
De-stress: relax and take care of your mind and body.	You feel stress all over your body, especially in your head. You draw pictures in your journal, and that relaxes you.

Ask for help from others: find people who can help you cope with your hurt.	You share with your best friend that your parents are stressing you out. She shares what is bothering her. You feel better just knowing that you are not the only one with hurt feelings.

Your buddy says, *"I will help you with your feelings of hurt so you don't have to be alone with them."*

Hurt Action Plan: The Three Ds

Step 1: *Describe* your hurt and the reason for it. (Look at activity 25 to remind yourself of some of the situations that might cause you to feel hurt.)

_____

_____

_____

_____

_____

_____

Step 2: *Decide* if the reason for your hurt is real by thinking for yourself.

	The idea is true	The idea is not true
Facts that show…		
Memories that show…		
Feelings I have that show…		
People who agree that…		
How I would feel if…		
People who would be mad if I believe…		

Circle your answer:

When I think for myself about the reason for my hurt, I realize that it is/is not real.

Using the Coping Tools

Step 3: *Dive* into your coping tools to help you with the situation.

Coping tool	What you have learned and what you plan to do
Consider your options: use STEP to see your choices	I choose this option:
Live your values	My core values that will help me are:
Act with courage	I will remind myself that I have courage by:
Encourage yourself	I will encourage myself by:
De-stress	I will de-stress by:
Ask for help from others	People who can help me are:

Your buddy says, *"Remember that you feel better when you deal with hurt. Coping with feelings helps you follow the rules for loving and feeling loved by both parents!"*

Confusion

What Is Confusion?

Confusion is a feeling kids get when they don't know what is right or true. They have a question but not an answer. If you are confused, you may feel like you are lost. You may have a hard time knowing what you feel or think. Confusion can happen when parents want you to do or say different things. It can make you feel a little crazy because you get all mixed up and don't know what to do or what to believe. You might get confused when your parents don't agree and each tries to get you on their side.

How Is Confusion Helpful?

Confusion tells you that there are two sides to something. Let's say you hear two different reasons from your parents for why they split up. You don't know who or what to believe. It's normal to be confused when stories aren't the same. Confusion tells you that you are unclear and need more facts to figure things out.

How Is Confusion a Problem?

Confusion is a problem when it makes you freeze up. Sometimes you can feel so lost and uncertain that you don't do anything, such as dive into your coping tools. You may even think that the confusion will go away if you choose one parent's side. Confusion makes it hard to love and feel loved by both parents.

Reasons for Your Confusion: Real or Not Real?

Did you know that feelings of confusion can come from reasons that are real and reasons that are not real? Even though your feeling of confusion is real, the reasons for it may not be. You can see if the reasons for the confusion are real or not by thinking for yourself. If you find that the reasons are not real, your body and muscles may relax and your feeling of confusion will probably go away. If you find that the reasons behind your confusion are real, you can use your coping tools to make an action plan.

Let's say that you feel confused because you think your teacher is fair, but your friend tells you that the teacher was mean to him. You don't know who to believe. You think for yourself and realize that the teacher has always been fair to you. You decide you aren't going to change your belief about the teacher based on what someone else tells you. Your coping tools help you figure out how to tell your friend that you aren't going to stop liking the teacher.

But what if after thinking for yourself you remember a time when the teacher spoke rudely to another student? You begin to wonder if maybe the teacher isn't as fair as you had thought. Now you can use your coping tools to figure out what to do about that.

Activity 30: What Does Confusion Feel Like?

In the sentences below, fill in the blank with a word that helps you learn something about confusion. (Your buddy has the answers for you on page 91.)

1. Your heart beats _____.

2. You feel like taking a _____ to have a break from thinking.

3. It's hard to _____ about anything else.

4. When you go to bed at night it may be hard to fall _____.

5. You don't want to eat since you have an upset _____.

6. You keep changing your _____ about what you think.

Has anyone ever told you that you look confused?   _____ yes   _____ no

If yes, write down how that person could tell. _____

_____

_____

(Hint: Look in the mirror the next time you feel confused and write down what you see.)

Using Coping Tools to Deal with Confusion

The coping tools from part 2 can help you deal with confusion. Here's how. Imagine you are dealing with situation number 3 from activity 25. Let's say your mom says something mean about your dad and hints that he is a bad person. You don't know whether it is true or not. You feel confused about whether or not your dad is bad.

Coping tools	Example
Think for yourself: decide whether the cause of your confusion is real.	You know your own truth about your dad. You know that he is a good person who loves you. You also realize that you are just a kid and can't really understand all the adult stuff about divorce.
Consider your options: use STEP to see your choices.	After using STEP you decide that you don't really understand what all the divorce stuff means. You decide not to listen to confusing grown-up stories about either parent.
Live your values: be clear about what you will and will not do.	Fairness is one of your core values. You decide not to take sides or listen to either parent say bad things about the other parent.
Act with courage: remember that you can be brave and do what is right.	You let your parents know that no matter how mad they are at each other, you don't want to take sides. You hope that they can see how important this is to you.
Encourage yourself: remind yourself that you can be okay with your confusion.	You remind yourself that you are just a kid and divorce is an adult problem. You don't have to figure out who is to blame. You don't have to take sides.
De-stress: relax and take care of your mind and body.	You feel tension all over your body, especially in your shoulders. You decide to read a good book in your favorite cozy reading spot. That helps you take your mind off of your parents' divorce.
Ask for help from others: find people who can help you cope with your confusion.	You talk to a teacher after school. She helps you figure out how to ask your parents to not say mean things about each other to you.

Your buddy says, *"Confusion doesn't feel good, but I can help you learn something helpful and important from it."*

(Answers to activity 30: 1. faster, 2. nap, 3. think, 4. asleep, 5. stomach, 6. mind)

Confusion Action Plan: The Three Ds

Step 1: *Describe* your confusion and the reason for it. (Look at activity 25 to remind yourself of some of the situations that might cause you to feel confused.)

_____

_____

_____

_____

_____

_____

Step 2: *Decide* if your confusion is real by thinking for yourself.

	The idea is true	The idea is not true
Facts that show…		
Memories that show…		
Feelings I have that show…		
People who agree that…		
How I would feel if…		
People who would be mad if I believe…		

Circle your answer:

When I think for myself about the reason for my confusion, I realize that it is/is not real.

Step 3: *Dive* into your coping tools to help you with the situation.

Coping tool	What you have learned and what you plan to do
Consider your options: use STEP to see your choices	I choose this option:
Live your values	My core values that will help me are:
Act with courage	I will remind myself that I have courage by:
Encourage yourself	I will encourage myself by:
De-stress	I will de-stress by:
Ask for help from others	People who can help me are:

Your buddy says, *"Remember that you make the best decisions when you can think clearly. When you deal with confusion, it's easier to follow the rules for loving and feeling loved by both parents!"*

Fear

What Is Fear?

Fear is a feeling you get when you are afraid. You might feel fear when your parents fight. You might fear that your parents are going to hurt one another or that one is going to leave. You might feel like you have to say things you don't believe for fear of making a parent mad.

How Is Fear Helpful?

Fear can help you stay safe. It tells you there is something you need to stay away from. Fear says, *Be careful*. In small amounts, fear can give you energy when you need it. It can also help you focus and think clearly. For example, when you are nervous in a school play or before a game, a little fear gives you energy and helps you focus.

When Is Fear a Problem?

Too much fear can stop you from taking action when you need to. It can freeze you in place. Fear can also keep you from thinking clearly or being able to focus. When you are taught to be afraid of something that isn't fearful, you can't always trust fear as a warning system. For example, if you were bitten by a little brown dog when you were younger, you might grow up to be afraid of all little brown dogs, even the nice ones.

Reasons for Your Fear: Real or Not Real?

Did you know that feeling afraid can come from reasons that are real and reasons that are not real? Even though your feeling of fear is real, the reasons for it may not be. You can see if the reasons for the fear are real or not by thinking for yourself. If you find that the reasons are not real, your body and muscles may relax and your fear will probably go away. If you find that the reasons behind your fear are real, you can use your coping tools to make an action plan.

Let's say your big brother tells you that the doctor is going to give you a super painful shot at your next appointment. After thinking for yourself you remember that you don't get a shot at every doctor visit, and even when you do the shot hurts only a little. You decide that most likely your brother is teasing you, and you use your coping tools to deal with that.

But suppose after thinking for yourself you do believe your brother, because he usually tells you the truth. He doesn't like to scare you for no reason. You can still use your coping tools to help you prepare for the painful shot.

Activity 31: What Does Fear Feel Like?

Fill in the blanks to learn more about what fear feels like in your body. Use one of these five words: tight, dry, sweaty, butterflies, tremble. (Your buddy has the answers on page 99.)

1. You feel like you have fluttery _____ in your stomach.

2. Your muscles are tense and _____.

3. You want a glass of water because your mouth feels so _____.

4. Your body might shake or _____.

5. You don't want to shake hands with anyone because your palms are so _____.

Has anyone ever told you that you look afraid?   _____ yes   _____ no

If yes, write down how that person could tell. _____

_____

_____

(Hint: Look in the mirror the next time you feel afraid and write down what you see.)

A Workbook for Children Coping with Divorce, Parental Alienation, and Loyalty Conflicts

Using Coping Tools to Deal with Fear

The coping tools from part 2 can help you deal with fear. Here's how. Imagine you are dealing with situation number 9 from activity 25. Let's say your dad tells you that your mom is a bad driver because she is angry and scary. He says that she is going to be in a car accident. To keep you safe, he wants you to tell people that you are afraid to be in the car with your mom.

Coping tools	Example
Think for yourself: decide whether the cause of your fear is real.	You realize that your mom has never had an accident or received a speeding ticket. You decide that you are probably safe in the car with her.
Consider your options: use STEP to see your choices.	After using STEP you decide that you have never felt afraid in the car with your mom. You wonder if your dad is just saying she's a bad driver because of the court stuff.
Live your values: be clear about what you will and will not do.	You value logic, and nothing tells you that your mom is an unsafe driver. You realize that you are safe in the car with her. You don't understand why your dad said that stuff, but you know that parents fight sometimes and say mean things about each other. You decide that you won't say you are afraid.
Act with courage: remember that you can be brave and do what is right.	You tell your dad that you think your mom is a safe driver and that you don't want to say anything that isn't true about either parent. You want to be left out of the divorce.
Encourage yourself: remind yourself that you can be okay with your fear.	You remind yourself that you feel safest when your parents get along. When they don't get along, you feel safest by staying out of their problems.
De-stress: relax and take care of your mind and body.	Your entire body feels stressed and tired. You decide to take a nap. Later you draw to relax and take your mind off your troubles.

Ask for help from others: find people who can help you cope with your fear.	You make an appointment to speak to the guidance counselor at school. You think that the counselor could really help you sort through your thoughts and feelings.

Your buddy says, *"Fear can feel scary in your mind and body, but you can handle it. Remember that I am here with you!"*

(Answers to activity 31: 1. butterflies, 2. tight, 3. dry, 4. tremble, 5. sweaty)

Fear Action Plan: The Three Ds

Step 1: *Describe* your fear and the reason for it. (Look at activity 25 to remind yourself of some of the situations that might cause you to feel fear.)

_____

_____

_____

_____

_____

_____

Step 2: *Decide* if the reason for your fear is real by thinking for yourself.

	The idea is true	The idea is not true
Facts that show…		
Memories that show…		
Feelings I have that show…		
People who agree that…		
How I would feel if…		
People who would be mad if I believe…		

Circle your answer:

When I think for myself about the reason for my fear, I realize that it is/is not real.

Using the Coping Tools

Step 3: *Dive* into your coping tools to help you with the situation.

Coping tool	What you have learned and what you plan to do
Consider your options: use STEP to see your choices	I choose this option:
Live your values	My core values that will help me are:
Act with courage	I will remind myself that I have courage by:
Encourage yourself	I will encourage myself by:
De-stress	I will de-stress by:
Ask for help from others	People who can help me are:

Your buddy says, *"You feel safest when you can trust your fear to warn you of danger. When you feel safe it's easier to follow the rules for loving and feeling loved by both parents!"*

Getting Through My Parents' Divorce

Guilt

What Is Guilt?

Guilt is a feeling you get when you think you have done something wrong. You might think that you have broken a rule or not lived up to your core values. Guilt feels heavy, like a burden you can't get rid of. Some people say that you feel guilt when you go against your conscience. "Conscience" is a name for the part of the mind that labels things as good or bad.

How Is Guilt Helpful?

Guilt can tell you when you have done something that you need to make right. It can help you know when you need to fix a relationship or change a behavior. Guilt can keep you from going against your values or doing something you know is wrong.

When Is Guilt a Problem?

Guilt can be false. If you believe you did something wrong when you didn't, that is false guilt. For example, if one parent doesn't want you to have a good time with the other parent, but you have a good time anyway, you might feel guilty. That is false guilt. If you don't deal with your guilt, you might start to think you are bad. Guilt can make you think you need to be punished when you haven't done anything wrong. It can make you believe that you should do things other people want you to do, even if you don't want to.

Reasons for Your Guilt: Real or Not Real?

Did you know that guilty feelings can come from reasons that are real and reasons that are not real? Even though your feeling of guilt is real, the reasons for it may not be. You can see if the reasons for the guilty feeling are real or not by thinking for yourself. If you find that the reasons are not real, your body and muscles may relax and your guilty feelings will probably go away. If you find that the reasons behind your guilt are real, you can use your coping tools to make an action plan.

Let's say that one of your friends wants you to tell a different friend that you don't want to be friends anymore. When you think about saying that to your other friend, you feel really guilty. After thinking for yourself you realize that the guilt is coming from your conscience. If you cut off a friend for no reason, you would be hurting that friend. You would not be living your values. You decide to say no to the friend who asked you to do something that you don't want to do.

Now the friend who asked you to cut off the other friend is mad at you, and you feel guilty. You think for yourself and decide that what you feel is false guilt. You use your coping tools to help you deal with the situation.

Activity 32: What Does Guilt Feel Like?

What does guilt feel like in your mind and body? Draw a picture of something you were doing the last time you felt guilty. Or draw a picture of something that you know would cause you to feel guilty.

Activity 33: Guilty Words

Circle these words in the word search to learn more about guilt. (Your buddy has the answers for you on page 109.)

nervous	anxious	betrayal
blush	fidgety	mad
sweaty	worried	

A	B	N	E	R	V	O	U	S	B	B	A	S	S
M	L	S	H	U	K	B	A	F	L	E	O	P	U
P	U	P	W	O	N	F	K	Q	R	T	P	D	O
B	S	I	Q	E	O	D	E	I	R	R	O	W	I
B	H	T	R	A	A	T	V	P	G	A	I	U	X
D	I	W	A	O	X	T	D	A	M	Y	N	M	N
N	F	I	D	G	E	T	Y	L	A	A	C	P	A
P	C	G	I	J	E	X	N	K	Q	L	C	B	M

Has anyone ever told you that you look guilty? _____ yes _____ no

If yes, write down how that person could tell. _____

_____

_____

(Hint: Look in the mirror the next time you feel guilt and write down what you see.)

Using Coping Tools to Deal with Guilt

The coping tools from part 2 can help you deal with guilt. Here's how. Imagine that you are dealing with situation number 13 in activity 25. Let's say that you have wanted to go to Disney World for a long time. Your mom tells you that she got tickets, but the trip falls on a weekend you are scheduled to be with your dad. She tells you to keep the trip a secret or your dad won't let you go. You really want to go on the trip, and you feel guilty when you see your dad and don't say anything about it.

Coping tools	Example
Think for yourself: decide whether the cause of your guilt is real.	After thinking for yourself you realize that your guilt is telling you that you are doing something wrong. It isn't false guilt. You realize that you shouldn't keep secrets from your parents about plans and schedules.
Consider your options: use STEP to see your choices.	After using STEP you decide that you don't want to keep the trip a secret, so you tell your dad about the plan. Then you feel guilty about doing what your mom asked you not to do. You know this is false guilt because it was wrong to ask you to keep the secret in the first place.
Live your values: be clear about what you will and will not do.	You value honesty. You decide that you are not going to be dishonest with either parent.
Act with courage: remember that you can be brave and do what is right.	You are nervous about telling your mom that you didn't keep the secret. You tell her in an e-mail because that feels better. You ask her to please not ask you to keep secrets, and you promise not to keep secrets with your dad either.
Encourage yourself: remind yourself that you can be okay with your guilt.	This secret business is confusing and getting you down. It's a lot of work to figure out the right thing to do. You feel proud that you know your values. You give yourself a pat on the back for doing the right thing, even though it was hard.

De-stress: relax and take care of your mind and body.	When you think about keeping secrets, you feel stress all over your body, especially in your head and throat. You decide to go outside for a walk because walking relaxes you.
Ask for help from others: find people who can help you cope with your guilt.	Your friend's mom and dad are friendly and kind. You decide to tell them that your parents are trying to get you involved in their divorce problems. They agree to help you figure out how to stay out of the middle, and they respect you for sharing your troubles with them.

Your buddy says, *"Guilt is hard to deal with because it could be true or false. It takes work to figure out, but I am here to help you."*

(Answers to activity 33)

A	B	N	E	R	V	O	U	S	B	B	A	S	S
M	L	S	H	U	K	B	A	F	L	E	O	P	U
P	U	P	W	O	N	F	K	Q	R	T	P	D	O
B	S	I	Q	E	O	D	E	I	R	R	O	W	I
B	H	T	R	A	A	T	V	P	G	A	I	U	X
D	I	W	A	O	X	T	D	A	M	Y	N	M	N
N	F	I	D	G	E	T	Y	L	A	A	C	P	A
P	C	G	I	J	E	X	N	K	Q	L	C	B	M

Guilt Action Plan: The Three Ds

Step 1: *Describe* your guilt and the reason for it. (Look at activity 25 to remind yourself of some of the situations that might cause you to feel guilt.)

_____

_____

_____

_____

_____

_____

Step 2: *Decide* if the reason for your guilt is real by thinking for yourself.

	The idea is true	The idea is not true
Facts that show…		
Memories that show…		
Feelings I have that show…		
People who agree that…		
How I would feel if…		
People who would be mad if I believe…		

Circle your answer:

When I think for myself about the reason for my guilt, I realize that it is/is not real.

Step 3: *Dive* into your coping tools to help you with the situation.

Coping tool	What you have learned and what you plan to do
Consider your options: use STEP to see your choices	I choose this option:
Live your values	My core values that will help me are:
Act with courage	I will remind myself that I have courage by:
Encourage yourself	I will encourage myself by:
De-stress	I will de-stress by:
Ask for help from others	People who can help me are:

Your buddy says, *"Remember, just because you feel like you have done something wrong doesn't mean that you have. When you deal with guilt, it's easier to follow the rules for loving and feeling loved by both parents!"*

To Help You Remember

You've come to the end of your workbook. Think of all you have learned!

You have new coping tools to help you love and feel loved by both parents. See if you can list all seven tools. (Hint: You used them in part 3 of the workbook.)

1. _____

2. _____

3. _____

4. _____

5. _____

6. _____

7. _____

Remember What Is Most Important

Draw a picture of yourself with both of your parents. The picture is yours to look at when you need help remembering the two of them with you. The picture is to remind you that it is okay for you to love both parents. Keep it with you in your backpack, take a picture of it with your cell phone, or keep a framed copy at both of your parents' houses. Or you can hold on to it in your mind. You can also ask your parents to take a photo with you.

Your buddy says, *"Good job! And remember, you are not alone."*

Amy J. L. Baker, PhD, is a national expert on parental alienation and has written a seminal book on the topic, *Adult Children of Parental Alienation Syndrome*, published by W. W. Norton &Company. In addition to conducting trainings around the country for parents as well as legal and mental health professionals, Baker has written dozens of scholarly articles on topics related to parent/child relationships and has appeared on national TV, including *Good Morning America*, CNN, and *The Joy Behar Show*. She has been quoted in *The New York Times* and *U.S. News & World Report*, among other print media outlets. Baker graduated from Barnard College, summa cum laude and Phi Beta Kappa. She has a PhD in human development from Teachers College, Columbia University.

Katherine C. Andre, PhD, is a licensed psychologist in clinical practice for over twenty years. She has worked extensively with families to prevent parental alienation before it begins and to strengthen parent/child relationships with both parents. As a court-appointed child custody director and mediator, she has supervised other mediators and helped parents to develop healthy parenting plans in their children's best interest. She holds a bimonthly class on parenting that teaches parents the importance of keeping their children out of conflict. She has published articles on parental alienation in the *Annals of the American Psychotherapy Association* and *The California Psychologist*, and has made contributions on parental alienation to other publications. She graduated from the College of William and Mary, and received her PhD from the University of Georgia with an area of specialization in child neuropsychology.